# TRY Me

## TODAY REMEMBER YOUR MAJOR EVOLUTION

## Latrice La'Shawn

TODAY REMEMBER YOUR MAJOR EVOLUTION

ISBN: 9798611244128

# *Dedication*

To all the trauma I have endured from those I love and loved dearly, I thank you. I believe in order to appreciate where you are you must embrace the journey that led you this far.

# Contents

# *Acknowledgments*

Litarsha Robinson,

You were the light during the darkest moments of my life. There are no words powerful enough to express my love and appreciation for you. Thank you for your guidance, I love you.

Alicia,

I think of you every day and admire your strength. You inspire me and make me whole. I pray God brings us together to experience a sisterhood like no other. I will never give up on you, my arms are open. I love you.

Aunt Stacy,

You were the epitome of the woman I strived to become. I have looked up to you since I was a little girl. I will forever love and appreciate you for setting an example for me and teaching me the greatest things in life come with time.

Nicole,

You have been there for me every step of the way and encouraged me to move forward with Try Me. I am not sure if I would have gotten this far without you. You were the bandage to my heart. You kept me together, focused, and because of it all, I too see my potential. I love you.

Ma,

I thank God for choosing you as my mother. Our relationship has blossomed through the course of time. I appreciate you for loving me the best way you knew how. You aided me in being my fullest self. Mommy I love you … Mommy I forgive you ♥

# *Introduction*

**T****oday Remember Your Major Evolution** and the reason why you are evolving. *Your Major Evolution* is the lesson within every tragedy during your stages of growth. Embrace the process and continue to be "a work in progress" in the process of becoming the greater person within you. *Remembering Your Major Evolution* is a pleasant reminder that alarms you anytime there are distractions or any chances of repeating the same mistakes. The moment you decide to break the barriers that kept you chained to the idea of not being enough, stay free, and love yourself more. When you start to love who you are and the person you are striving to become, I promise you, the things and people you thought were important will not have the power to disrupt your peace. You will become more inclined to finding solutions rather than adding more to the problem.

My biggest problem was having expectations of others. When there is an expectation, you are leaving room for disappointment. Expecting loyalty, respect, love, and bond for those you care for I thought was a given. However, in reality, people are people; blood is not always thicker than water, and time does not determine the amount of respect and loyalty a person should receive. I still struggle with this, longing to fix the unfixable with people who do not see the damage nor the need for repair. It has taken some time to realize the amount of control I have over my life.

That realization led me to share the experiences that helped shape me into the woman I am today. Truth is, I still battle with depression, anger, and at times can be resentful. Truth is, I am better today than I was days, months, and years ago. I have built a wall so strong and so high that it will take years to break down. Those walls were built from years of trauma, heartbreak, and pain.

So, I decided to take control of my life and do whatever it took to become the woman God destined for me to become. In the midst of the weathered storm, I came across the light of the sun that shines on my reality, brightens my day, and gives me hope and helps to build my faith. I felt freedom within the wind; free to love who I am right now despite the blemishes of my past that still bring back those memories. Let's not forget that one cloud that always has a 50% chance of rain. But not all rain is a burden; at times it washes the pain away and waters the depth of my soul to break through the cracks, just like a concrete rose. I have noticed many of us are scared to grow because we are afraid; we may outgrow somethings and the people we thought were bigger than ourselves. Truth is, our plans are not always the plans God has for our lives. He may take you through some things for you to see for yourself. We must learn to see the potential within ourselves and not seek validation from others. It is important to know what works for you. *Try Me* in this.

I will change if I must,
slow my life down to readjust
from being an aunt to mothering you
because I love you that much.

# 1

## Motherless Child

Growing up as the youngest child on both sides of my family, I had an expectation of my older siblings to teach and protect me. In reality, the idea of what a family is "*supposed*" to do does not relate to everyone. Family is *supposed* to be supportive and love one another; however, every experience does not leave you with the *supposing* feeling. At a young age, my sister started using drugs. Given the absence of her mother and the inconsistent presence of my father, who was there during times of his freedom, she did not have a healthy support system or guidance. She would go missing for months and be on the streets strung out in need of money for food or her next high. So, she started to prostitute herself and became pregnant. My niece was born prematurely and was taken by the child protective services due to drugs being within her body. My father adopted my niece and eventually gained full custody. At that moment, I felt like a mini mommy. I felt like God gave my sister someone to live for, someone to love. This was her major evolution. With all the tragedies my sister was experiencing, I thought maybe this was

her opportunity to break away from the streets. Instead, my sister was not ready to take on the responsibility of her unexpected blessing.

I loved her so much that I started to build my life, pursuing things that will help me help her. *Try Me* was founded to shine a light on women who have dealt with similar situations and doing whatever it took to overcome their experiences and past. With hope, it will grasp the attention of my sister and influence her to get help and treatment. Yet, you can only do but so much at the age of a young teen. With that being said, it is not our job to please our family, especially if we can barely please ourselves. Often times, we look for acceptance from others, like how I looked for approval from my sister. I wanted and expected things that she was incapable of giving me at that stage of her life, that being sisterhood. Despite the pressure I felt to become a role model for my niece, I appreciated the challenge and even the obligations that were required because of my sister's absence.

So, what do you do when you are related and not quite relatable? The constant accusations of not understanding her pain and accusing me of believing that I was better than her without trying to see us as equals, made me feel abandoned and unappreciated. Meanwhile, she became a spectator to a story she did not know, and it caused more animosity towards me. Hearing the words, "I never liked you since we were little," are the words she would say easily. When my father and I would have disagreements, he would share and express his side to my sister, leaving room for her to form more opinions. I decided to keep trying to reconcile our relationship and was there to support her when she was released from jail after serving over four years. A little time after her release, she went back to using drugs and had another baby. She wanted another shot at motherhood, and I was not allowed to meet my newborn niece.

The decisions people make for themselves are simply their decisions. Whatever happens as a result of their decisions is NOT YOUR FAULT! God tested my strength endlessly because every situation could have been worse. The greatest fights are given to the toughest soldiers. As you are evolving, you will no longer see things how you did during times of confinement. You will subconsciously find your HOW within every situation. "How can I fix this?" "If I do this, how will it affect me?" "How do I move forward without return?" All you have been through becomes a part of you, and to move forward, you must find your lesson in every experience and not allow it to live on through your journey. It is easier said than done, right?

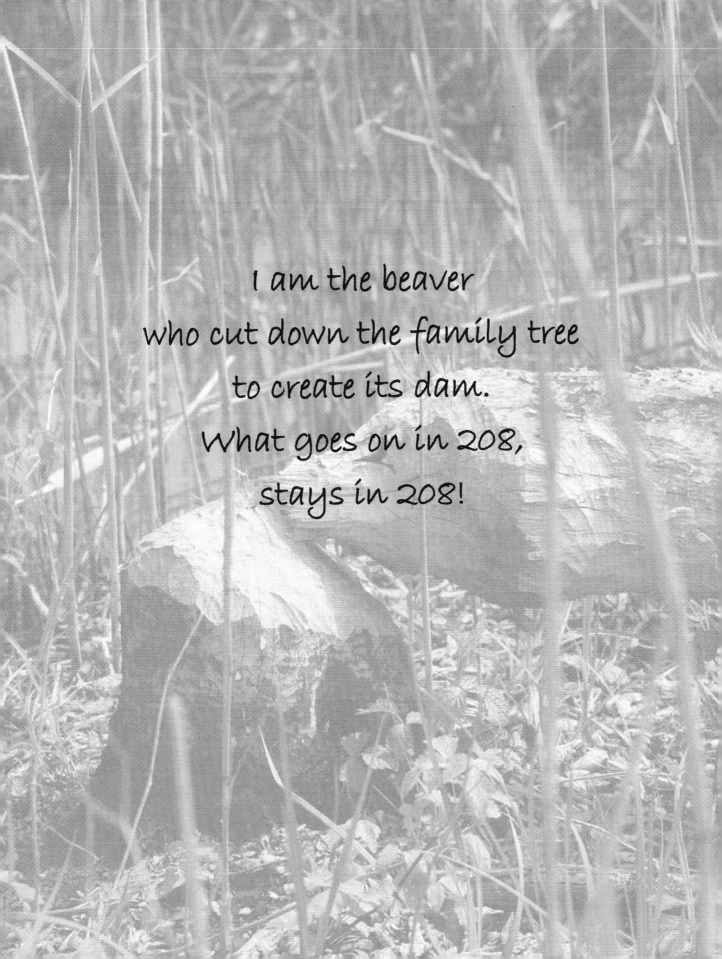

I am the beaver
who cut down the family tree
to create its dam.
What goes on in 208,
stays in 208!

# 2

## *Beaver*

Your parents are your first teachers, and I was taught to be silent. I appeared to be a happy child who was talented and did well in school. I was the cool kid. But within, I was confused, depressed, and hurting. I participated in every after-school activity because walking up the alley way towards 208 N. Gilmor Street was like walking into a horror-filled scenario of what if's and maybes of personal dangers. Yet, it was in my home that I became a BEAVER. I was the beaver who cut down the family tree and destroyed the potential bond I could have had with my mother because I refused to let the deep-rooted traditions of secretive silence continue to grow.

*"Whatever happens in my house stays in my house!*
*And you'd betta not tell a soul!"*

This is the phrase many families have heard from generation to generation. We hear many women answer quickly to what they would or would not do if they were put into a harmful situation with responses like, "I wish somebody would!" or "I'd never let that happen." However, one can never truly predict their actions, no matter how confident they are in their positive morals and beliefs until faced with unimaginable circumstances.

I was molested and abused as a child by my mother's ex-boyfriend, **Beaver.** One day she caught him violating me and simply stated, "Do not do that." His explanation was he was teaching me how to French kiss. She did nothing to protect me. I am not sure if she knew how. I knew as a little girl if I told my father he would have spent the rest of his life in a prison cell. I used my weekend getaways with my father as an escape from being at a place I thought was home. Just when I thought it would stop there, more shit happened, leaving me with more to figure out. I started to question my sexuality. During the times of my father's absence in prison, my mother allowed Beaver's cousin to stay at the house to attend school during the week and sent me over to her home on the weekends. One day she violated me leaving me to cry to my mom and told her that I was not gay. She stopped staying at the house not because she violated me but because Beaver victimized her.

What I am about to reveal reminds me of the story of the Little Boy Who Cried Wolf. She was a misunderstood girl who was troubled and mature for her age. She lied about things so much that no one ever believed anything she said. But on this day, she had a witness. She cried and said Beaver, her cousin, made her touch his penis. I walked into my room and saw Beaver pulling up his pants in front of her, and in shock, I quickly shut the door. Seconds later, he left my room, went back into my mother's bedroom, and shut the door. When she told her mom, her mother assumed she was lying because she did not want to stay there. When I told my mother, she convinced me that he would never do anything to hurt "us." Unfucking believable!

# BEAVER

Listen, I went to the extreme to get this man out of the house. As a kid, I was transferred to Harlem Park Elementary School, and during lunchtime they sold fresh baked cookies. I used to take money from my mother's black leather pouch to buy cookies, with hopes she would suspect Beaver was stealing her money. Beaver did not have a job and did drugs, so it wasn't hard to believe. Funny thing she never doubted me, but it didn't work. Damn! It was at that very moment I realized Beaver was my mother's happiness and nothing could come between or jeopardize that, not even me.

> *"People will do what's best for them at the moment until what's best for them is no longer best."*

From that moment on, I blamed everyone. From that moment on, I was numb. From that moment on, I was lost. And from that moment on, my barriers grew bigger. As I got older, it affected me more because I was able to put into perspective what happened to me. Happiness became a challenge because I did not know how to receive love and care. It is not easy to let go and forgive, especially when those you expect to love and protect you, view what is morally wrong as "not that serious." I felt as if I was not chosen or worthy of being loved and protected. I wanted to be accepted and as my mother's child, I thought it was a given. My mother chose her happiness over the safety of her children. If happiness was so important, I wanted to know what it felt like. Ironically, I could never be happy in the midst of rejection, family secrets, and dysfunctional relationships. I knew to be truly happy; I may have to isolate myself from my family. Instead, for many years, I took the punches of allowing everyone to believe that I was the problem. I kissed ass to fit into a family where I never felt welcomed. I convinced myself that I was misunderstood.

> *"When you feel tangled, unravel yourself
> from all the chaos that kept you bound."*

This tragic experience taught me to love myself even more. Know that somethings that are bigger than you will try to come in between you and your destiny. Though you may be present or aware of a situation, it doesn't mean you have experienced true peace and victory. For you to be completely free, you must go back, confront those responsible for the situation and embrace the truth. Do not allow the hurts and betrayals of your past to be a welcome guest in your future. With time I learned the greatest peace and loyalty comes by accepting people for who they are without trying to change them into what you expect them to be.

I witnessed my mom go above and beyond for her significant other. I have concluded a man will do what you allow him to do. I believe if you are dating someone with kids, you date the kids too. Help me understand, how can a man live under your roof and go grocery shopping for only himself, knowing you have kids to feed? So yes, I would eat his food, drink his juice, his soda and ate the snacks too. If I was hungry, I ate. I've never been to prison, but I'm sure it wasn't much different from living in a home with food and being told you couldn't eat it because it belongs to the "man" of the house. People would always tell me to mind my business and to let my mother live her life. You know I felt like my mother was my business and regardless of what happened, she is my mother whom I love very much, and no one could come in between that. I pray I learn to forgive; I am working on it.

# Sleeping with The Enemy

# 3

## *Fat Fat*

As he choked me, I was fighting to breathe; fighting for him to let go! I remember feeling weak and eventually stopped fighting back. Tears were rolling down my face as I struggled to cry out his roommate's name for help. In response, all I heard was a pause on his roomie's tv and as the roommate did nothing more than listen. As I fought back, the physical abuse got worse and worse. The next day I woke up with carpet burns from being dragged across the floor, blood clots in my eyes, a busted lip, and bruises all over my body. I disguised it all with a funny story of how I fell and enjoyed wearing long sleeve jackets in the summertime.

I isolated myself from everything and everyone. There were a select few who knew of my situation and befriended me because of it. Close friends felt as if I was putting their lives in jeopardy and chose not to get involved because I kept going back. Why, you may ask? **He validated that I was someone worthy to love.** I did not love myself enough to protect myself. He came into my life during a time I needed comfort,

during the time I was dealing with the trauma from my past and the disconnected relationship I had with my mother, he too was my scapegoat. I loved him so much that I ignored the truth about him. He would make little jokes about how I was not to look in a particular direction if a man was standing nearby. He would engage in playful talks about smacking me for talking back to him and how I belong to him. These were the signs I ignored and chose to stay.

I was the *"I would never take shit from anyone"* type of woman until I got lost in the lies and began to accept the abnormal as normal. I have witnessed toxic relationships from the people who surrounded me. I never witnessed nor was taught what a healthy relationship felt or looked like. I should have learned what not to allow when it came to relationships. Yet, I have realized that with even knowing better, the person must be ready to do better. Despite the various love notes he left on my car and my front door, I finally decided to ignore his advances and took action to press charges against him. Internal Affairs picked up my case, and I found out that I was not the only person this "officer" used as a punching bag, nor was I the last. He was given numerous opportunities to rehabilitate himself, yet he refused to change, and all he got was a long-term suspension as a result of my case. What if the bottle he swung would have landed on my head? What if he decided to use the gun he kept under his pillow?

> Never put your life in danger because you are looking for someone to love you.

I have chosen not to revisit every incident of domestic abuse I have experienced because regardless of the circumstances, it is never an excuse for a man to hit a woman or vice versa. So, yea, he called me *Fat Fat,* and we had a very destructive relationship. This led to the start of my excessive drinking, constant car crashes, and going out seven days a week. Yet this same man showed up amid my struggle and shortcomings to offer me what I thought was love and support. Have you ever had someone come into your life with the solution to all your problems, and it turned out to be your worst nightmare and felt like the greatest blessing? When I came to my senses, I questioned if this was God's way of testing my strength or showing me that all things that appear healthy aren't so good after all. It took everything to be taken away from me for me to see that new favor needed to be released within my life. These events led to me finding my purpose. There is no greater love than the love that you give to yourself.

I remember first meeting him through a mutual friend. Ladies just a quick note, it is something about a man who loves taking a woman to the "spot" where he's known or is there too often with a new woman every week. I don't know what it is. It's like the warm welcomes when you walk in the door or not having to pay at the door that strokes their ego or makes them feel like big shit when 9 times out of 10, they're not shit at all, don't fall for it.

I remember the night I was drunk after leaving the hookah bar, he was supposed to take me home. I fell asleep in the car and woke up as he was parking his car in his apartment's parking lot. I questioned, "Where am I?" and having the urge to use the bathroom, I proceeded in his home. After using the bathroom, I asked if he was ready to take me home. He started to kiss me and basically told me that I was going to give him "some." I said no and asked if he would stop, but next thing I knew I was pushed on the bed, and we were having sex. And the next day, I received a text after I was dropped off, asking if we were together. I don't know what I thought or was thinking, but the relationship then began. Now to this day I ask myself, was I raped? Was I too soft-spoken? Did I really want this to happen? This was actually the first time I witnessed his aggression, and I ignored it.

No one should go through the fire just for a person to see their worth. Just when I thought I despised him; I forgave him for his mistakes until I realized they were choices that were being made. I made a vow to put myself first and settle for no one! At times when I think of all the things I tolerated; I thank God I found myself in time. And just like that I became a new person that even I didn't know.

# A Note to You

Only I could narrate my story, so I decided to become an author. I hope that after reading this book, you are inspired to heal your open wounds and move pass anything that hinders you from moving forward towards what God has destined for you. I never knew I would reach this level of peace, so I decided to give my life to Christ. Even though I am not perfect and still struggle with many things, it is such a secure feeling to know that I have a Protector in my life who loves me unconditionally, gives endless chances and has a purpose for me to help people. Sharing my story was not the easiest thing to do, but it created a voice I never knew I had and allows me to help you. Try Me in this, always love you more.

# About the Author

There is never an ending to a story of a woman with imperfections. The most beautiful thing about a woman is the blemishes that create her new beginnings for each chapter of her life. Latrice Hayes is the founder of Try Me LLC, a movement created to represent women who are turning and have turned their tragedies into triumphs. She is a Baltimore, MD native, who inspires to bring women together collectively to experience a healing journey together as one. She is a graduate of the prestigious Morgan State University Business School and currently pursuing her Masters in Human Services within the collaborative program at Coppin State University and the University of Baltimore. Latrice aspires to motivate women to be the best version of themselves.

Made in the USA
Middletown, DE
12 May 2022

65676140R00018